First published in Great Britain 1977 by Ward Lock Ltd.
Copyright © 1977 by Grisewood & Dempsey Ltd.
All rights reserved. a b c d e f g h
This edition is published by Derrydale, a division of
Crown Publishers, Inc.
Printed in Singapore by Tien Wah Press (Pte) Ltd.

Library of Congress Cataloging in Publication Data

Rowland-Entwistle, Theodore.
  Let's look at wild animals.

  Includes index.
  SUMMARY: Describes briefly the characteristics and
natural environment of a variety of wild animal groups
including the big cats, monkeys and apes, and bears.
  1. Animals--Juvenile literature. [1. Animals]
I. Atkinson, Mike. II. Justice, Jennifer L.
III. Title. IV. Title: Wild animals.
QL49.R67 1979   591   79-84412
ISBN 0-517-28728-5

LET'S LOOK AT
WILD ANIMALS

Written by Theodore Rowland-Entwistle

Illustrated by Mike Atkinson

Edited by Jennifer Justice

DERRYDALE · NEW YORK

tiger

serval

The serval lives in Africa. It climbs trees, and can spring up to catch a bird 6 feet (2 meters) above ground.

Tigers like the one on the left used to live in many parts of Asia. Today they are in danger of dying out because people have taken their hunting grounds for farmland. A tiger needs a very large area to hunt in. It kills about 43 deer, cattle, and other animals a year.

jaguar

saber-toothed tiger

The Big Cats

The cats that share our homes are small members of a whole family of cats. We call the largest members, such as lions and tigers, the "big cats." But even these huge beasts are not as big as the saber-toothed tiger, which roamed North America when our ancestors lived in caves. It is called "saber-toothed" because it had two very long teeth shaped like sabers (curved swords) in its upper jaw.

A fully-grown lion or tiger can weigh twice as much as a heavyweight boxer. Despite its size, the tiger is not often seen in the wild. Its striped coat makes it difficult to see in long grass. In the same way a lion's tawny coat helps to hide it in the dusty grasslands where it lives. Most members of the cat family are much smaller than lions and tigers. One of the smallest, other than the domestic cat, is the wildcat of western Europe, which is not much bigger than a domestic tabby cat.

The jaguar is the largest of the American cats. It lives in forests as far south as Argentina and as far north as Mexico. Jaguars are very good climbers. They sometimes lie hidden in trees, waiting to catch tree-living animals. Like tigers, jaguars enjoy swimming. They catch fish and even small alligators. And like most cats, jaguars usually sleep by day and hunt by night.

The leopard lives in southern Asia and most of Africa. It has a yellowish coat covered with dark spots. In Asia some leopards have almost black coats. They are called panthers.

leopard

A leopard often carries its prey up a tree. There it will be out of the way of scavengers such as jackals.

The fastest runner in the animal kingdom is the cheetah. It reaches speeds of over 60 mph (100 km/hr) on the open grasslands of Africa where it lives. The cheetah catches its prey by running after it and springing on its back.

You have probably noticed that a cat can draw in its claws, pulling them up and back so that they do not scratch you. All other members of the cat family except the cheetah can do this. The cheetah, like the dog, has blunt claws that do not draw back, or retract.

cheetah

Lionesses do most of the hunting and looking after the cubs. But sometimes a male lion will let the cubs come close to play.

male lion

The bone and muscle of a cat's toe, showing how the claw retracts.

lion cubs

Fleet-footed Grazers

Africa's wide grasslands are home for more large wild animals than any other part of the world. Huge herds of grazing animals still roam there despite the work of hunters. Some of these herds are several thousand strong. They wander slowly over the plains, though they can run swiftly when they are in danger. Several kinds of animals can live together in the same area because they do not all eat the same food. Gazelles like to eat tender young shoots of grass. Zebras prefer their grass longer and tougher.

The biggest herds are found in the moist grasslands, where there are plenty of waterholes for them to drink at. There you will find zebras, gnus and waterbucks. In the dry grasslands live small herds of animals that can go a long time without a drink, such as gazelles. Thorny trees and bushes provide food for animals that can reach up high to eat, such as the long-necked giraffe and the gerenuk, which can stand on its hind legs. The little dik-dik eats the lower-growing leaves.

The giraffe uses its long tongue to curl around leaves and carefully pull them out from among the thorns.

giraffe

rhinoceros

gerenuk

dik-dik

The grazing animals have several dangerous enemies. Lions, leopards, cheetahs, hyenas and wild dogs all stalk the herds, hoping to make a kill.

When they see an enemy such as a cheetah approaching, the grazing animals turn and run. The strongest escape, but any that are ill or weak are caught. In this way Nature makes sure that only the best animals survive.

Lions hunt by themselves or in small groups. Leopards and cheetahs work on their own. Wild dogs form packs of 50 or more. The grazing animals fear them most of all.

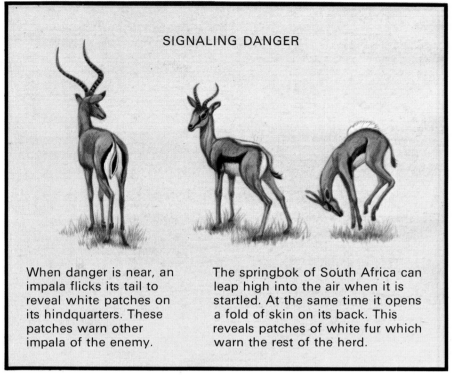

SIGNALING DANGER

When danger is near, an impala flicks its tail to reveal white patches on its hindquarters. These patches warn other impala of the enemy.

The springbok of South Africa can leap high into the air when it is startled. At the same time it opens a fold of skin on its back. This reveals patches of white fur which warn the rest of the herd.

Zebras are very close relatives of horses and donkeys. Their black and white stripes help to hide them from their main enemy, the lion. At a distance the stripes blend with the tall grasses and make the zebras very hard to see.

zebra

impala

cheetah

Swamps and Rivers

Many big animals live in the swamps and rivers of Africa. The biggest is the hippopotamus, which is one of the heaviest of all land animals. The name hippopotamus means "water horse." A hippo likes to spend most of the day under water, with only its eyes and nostrils showing. It swims well, and walks on its toes on the river bed. It comes ashore at night to feed.

Another large animal is the Nile crocodile, which is the nearest living relative of the great dinosaurs of prehistoric times. Crocodiles spend much of their time in water to keep cool. They eat fish and any other unwary animals that come near them. But they often allow birds to perch on them. The birds help the crocodiles by pecking at the tiny insects on the crocodiles' backs.

kingfisher

pelican

hippopotamus

jacana

Several big relatives of the crocodile live in the Americas. The alligator looks very like a crocodile, and grows nearly as big. It lives in the swamps in the southeastern United States. Using its spade-like feet and its thrashing tail an alligator digs a deep hole to live in. This alligator hole makes a pond home for many other animals, such as fish, frogs, turtles and snakes.

Female alligators build large mounds of mud and sticks in which to lay their eggs. Groups of these nests sometimes form islands in the swamp on which trees grow.

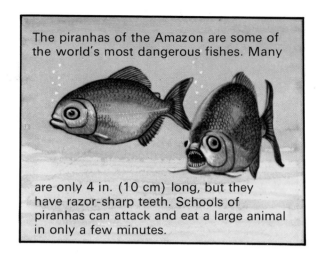

The piranhas of the Amazon are some of the world's most dangerous fishes. Many are only 4 in. (10 cm) long, but they have razor-sharp teeth. Schools of piranhas can attack and eat a large animal in only a few minutes.

In Central and South America you will find the caimans, cousins of the alligator. The biggest is the black caiman, which lives in the Amazon region of Brazil. There is also an American crocodile, closely related to the Nile crocodile. Its head is longer and narrower than an alligator's.

gharial

The gharial lives in the big rivers of India, Pakistan, Bangladesh and Burma. It has a very long, thin snout which it uses to seize fish. It is not dangerous to humans.

spectacled caiman

The spectacled caiman gets its name from the bony ridges on its head, which look like a pair of glasses. It is normally a shy animal, but a female caiman will defend her nest fiercely against attackers.

raccoon

green tree frog

green snake

cottonmouth

American alligator

painted turtle

11

Hunters and Scavengers

Have you ever wondered what happens to the remains of a lion's dinner? Or what happens to the bodies of animals that die naturally? They are all tidied up by a group of very useful animals known as scavengers. Some scavengers such as vultures live only on dead animals. They never kill their own food. Hyenas are scavengers, but they kill as well.

Many of the hunting animals are watched closely by scavengers. The puma, or mountain lion, is a very wasteful hunter. It often kills far more animals than it needs for food. In this way it provides a free meal for other hunters and scavengers. When the larger scavengers have eaten their fill, smaller ones move in. Many insects, especially beetles, feed on carrion (dead flesh) until only the clean bones are left behind.

Pumas and other big cats usually hunt on their own. Other animals form packs to look for food. Wolves hunt together in this way. They never seem to get tired, and often chase their prey for hours until it drops.

The hyenas of Africa and southern Asia also hunt in packs. They prowl at night, barking harshly or making sounds like wild laughter. Hyenas often eat a lion's leftovers, but sometimes a lion will drive a pack of hyenas away from an animal they have killed. The lion then acts as scavenger, and eats the hyenas' leftovers!

The puma hunts by night. It creeps up on its prey and then pounces. It is also called the cougar, the catamount and the mountain lion. It looks like a small lioness.

In spite of its size and its dangerous antlers, a caribou is no match for a pack of wolves.

The Andean condor is a huge vulture that lives high up in the Andes Mountains of South America. Its wingspan is twice the width of a small car.

Dingoes are the wild dogs of Australia. They are descended from tame dogs taken there thousands of years ago. They hunt in small family groups, and chase and catch wallabies (small kangaroos). Dingoes are often shot because they attack sheep.

Vultures flock around a dead animal and soon tear it to pieces. They are fierce birds and have been known to drive a cheetah away from its kill. Vultures can spot "meals" from high in the sky.

The coyote lives in the western part of North America. Its sad howl can be heard a long way away.

The spotted hyena has very strong jaws that can crush animal bones to get at the soft marrow inside.

Tropical Rain Forest

In the tropics, the hot parts of the world near the Equator, are the rain forests. They are called rain forests because they grow where the climate is always wet. Most of the trees are very tall, with bare trunks and a crown of leaves far above the ground. Only a little light comes through the leaves, and it is always gloomy on the forest floor. Very few low-growing plants can survive in the rain forest. There are not very many big animals, because there is little food for them at ground level. But high up

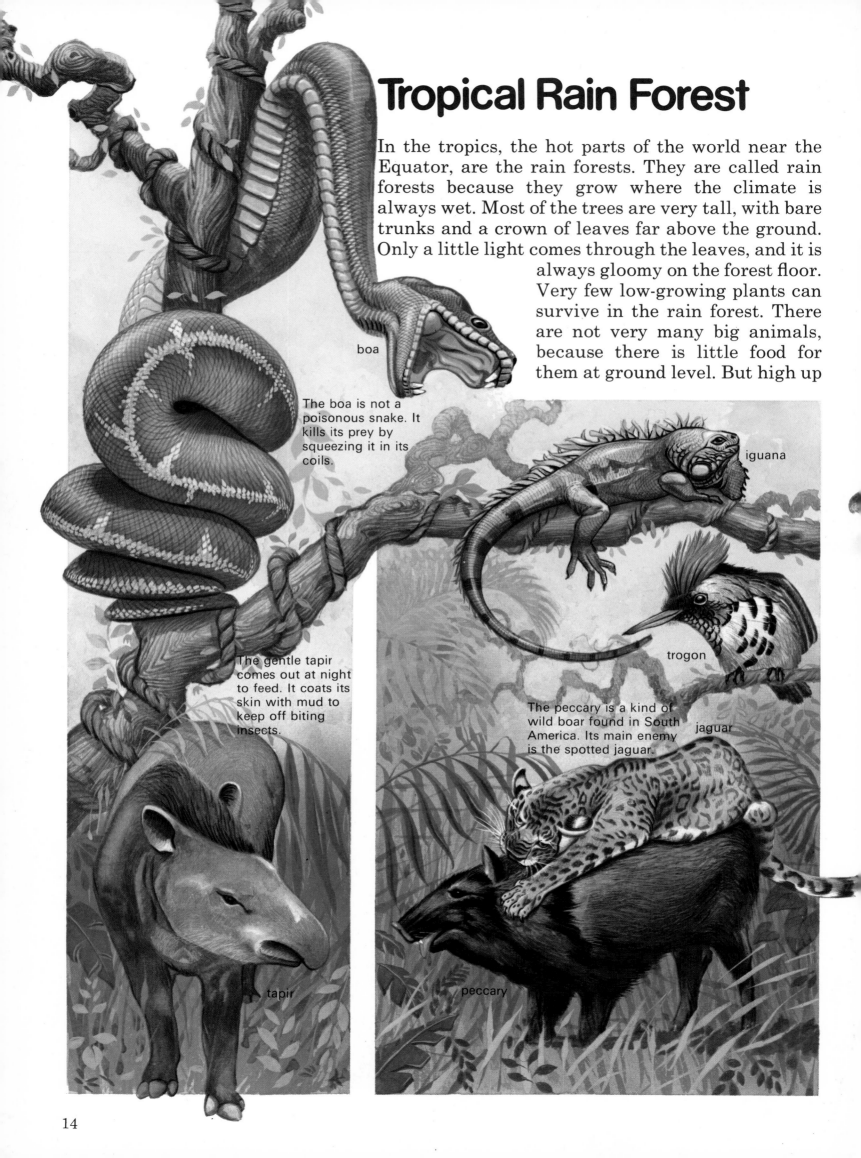

boa

The boa is not a poisonous snake. It kills its prey by squeezing it in its coils.

iguana

trogon

The gentle tapir comes out at night to feed. It coats its skin with mud to keep off biting insects.

The peccary is a kind of wild boar found in South America. Its main enemy is the spotted jaguar.

jaguar

tapir

peccary

in the trees many different animals make their homes and find their food. The forest is noisy with the chatter and cries of monkeys, swinging from branch to branch in search of fruit and nuts. Almost as noisy are the colorful parrots, which fly in flocks from one tree to another. Snakes slither along the branches or through the leaves on the ground.

In South American rain forests lives the slow-moving sloth, which spends almost all its time hanging upside-down from a branch. Lower down, the coatimundi, a relative of the raccoon, hunts for lizards and birds. The jaguar's spots help to hide it as it stalks its prey.

bats

cock-of-the-rock

three-toed sloth

The three-toed sloth is called the *ai* because of the sad noise it makes.

woolly monkey

coatimundi

anteater

The giant anteater uses its sharp claws to tear open ants' nests. It catches ants with its sticky tongue.

gorillas

chimpanzee

Many monkeys like high living – they spend their whole lives in the trees. Among these tree-dwellers is the long-haired colobus monkey with its beautiful silky coat. Another high-flyer is the dainty Diana monkey, which spends most of its time in the very tops of the trees, where the fruit it likes to eat grows.

colobus monkey

Diana monkey

mandrill

Monkeys and Apes

Monkeys and apes are the animals that look rather like us. Scientists believe that Man and the monkeys and apes have a common ancestor which lived millions of years ago. Apes are the most like us; they have no tails and their brains are more like ours.

There are four kinds of ape – the gibbons and orang-utans which live in Asia, and the gorillas and chimpanzees which live in Africa. The gorilla is the biggest of the apes, and the chimpanzee is the most intelligent.

Most monkeys have human-like "hands." Unlike other animals, a monkey has a thumb opposite its other fingers. The thumb makes it possible for it to catch hold of objects, such as fruit and branches. Monkeys are expert climbers and gymnasts. Most use their tails for balancing, but nearly all South American monkeys have prehensile tails. This means that they can use their tails to hold onto things, like an extra hand.

The orangutan lives on the islands of Borneo and Sumatra. Its name means "man of the woods."

orangutan

monkey-eating eagle

One of the monkey's most dangerous enemies is the monkey-eating eagle.

termite nest

chimpanzee

Chimpanzees can use simple tools. This one is using a stick to poke termites out of their mud nest.

The gibbon (right) has very long arms. It can swing from branch to branch through the trees without using its feet. Its hand has very long, flexible fingers. The hand at the top of the picture is that of an orangutan. As you can see, the hands of apes and monkeys are very like our own.

gibbon

orangutan's hand

gibbon's hand

baboons

Unlike so many other monkeys, baboons (right) and their cousins the mandrills (left) spend most of their lives on the ground. They live in large groups in rocky and grassy parts of Africa. Like all monkeys and apes, baboons spend a lot of time grooming – picking through each other's fur to remove dirt and insects, such as fleas. This grooming is a sign of friendship.

Beating the Heat

The word "desert" often makes us think of a dry, sandy place with no plants or life of any kind. Some deserts really are like that – parts of the Sahara, for example, and southern Arabia. But many deserts are home for a large number of living creatures. Such places include the deserts of North America. In summer the American deserts are burned almost bare by the fierce sun, and the ground is so hot you could fry an egg on it. Yet the animals and plants that live there all have ways of beating the heat to stay alive.

Among the plants that can stand the heat of the desert are cactuses. When it rains, they store water in their fleshy stems. They have no leaves through which to lose moisture.

Most of the animals that live in the desert keep out of the hot sun during the day in holes underground. They come out to feed at night, when it is cool. One of these is the horned toad – which is really a lizard. Its color is the same as its surroundings. It feeds on insects and other small creatures, such as spiders.

Some desert animals, such as the tiny kangaroo rat and the larger jack rabbit, get their water from the plants they eat. They in turn are eaten by animals such as snakes, falcons and foxes. These animals get the water they need from the bodies of their prey.

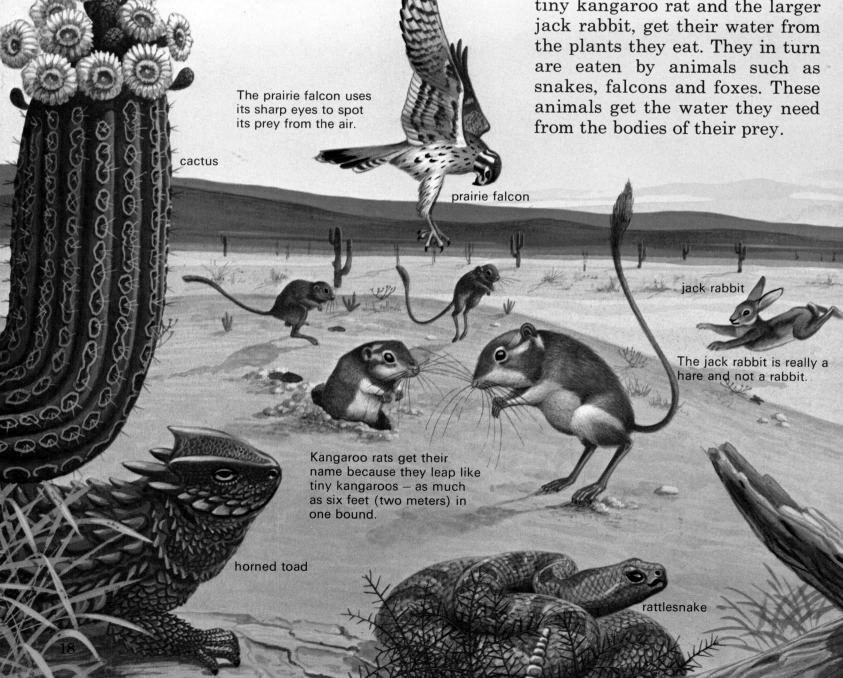

cactus

The prairie falcon uses its sharp eyes to spot its prey from the air.

prairie falcon

jack rabbit

The jack rabbit is really a hare and not a rabbit.

Kangaroo rats get their name because they leap like tiny kangaroos – as much as six feet (two meters) in one bound.

horned toad

rattlesnake

trapdoor spider

THE HIDDEN TRAP
The trapdoor spider is a kind of small tarantula that lives in a hole in the ground. It lines its tunnel with silk and makes a hinged lid of the same material. The spider covers the lid with sand so that it matches the ground. When an insect passes, the spider leaps out to grab it.

ONE HUMP OR TWO?
The camel is a desert animal of Africa and Asia. The Bactrian camel has two humps. A few still live wild in the Gobi Desert of Central Asia. The Arabian camel has one hump. Camels can go for long periods without eating or drinking. With their broad, padded feet they can walk easily over hot, dry sand.

Arabian camel

Bactrian camel

A WARNING RATTLE
A rattlesnake's rattle is made up of a series of horny plates which fit loosely together. The snake "rattles" these plates when it is frightened or angry.

cactus

kit fox

The kit fox has large ears, which help it to lose heat and so keep it cool.

The hairy tarantula kills its victims with its poisonous bite.

The scorpion is a relative of the spider. Its tail carries a poisonous sting.

scorpion

tarantula

grasshopper

pack rat

Giants of the Land

Elephants are the biggest animals that live on land. There are two kinds, the African elephant and the Asian elephant. A large African elephant stands twice as tall as a man and weighs as much as seven family cars.

The elephant's long trunk acts as a hand as well as a nose. It is very strong. With its trunk an elephant can pick up a heavy log or push over a wooden fence. Yet it can also use it for very delicate tasks, like picking up a peanut.

female elephant

When a baby elephant is born it looks tiny beside its mother. Yet it weighs as much as a heavyweight boxer.

A baby elephant can stand up a few minutes after it is born, and can walk within an hour. It is grown-up at 11 years old, though it goes on getting bigger.

An elephant mother takes great care of her child. Often an elephant "aunt" – a female without a baby of her own – helps her to look after her offspring. Mother and aunt take turns guarding the baby, which might otherwise be trampled underfoot in the herd.

African elephants

A fully-grown elephant has two long ivory tusks, one on each side of its trunk. These tusks are really extra-long teeth. The elephant uses them for lifting and fighting.

An elephant's right-hand tusk is usually shorter than the left-hand one. It is worn down because the elephant uses it more. Like people, elephants are more often right-handed than left-handed!

People have hunted elephants for thousands of years – all because of their tusks. Each tusk is a mass of solid ivory. People use ivory for carving, and to make such things as knife-handles.

To protect elephants from hunters, thousands are now kept in wildlife parks in Africa. Their numbers are slowly increasing.

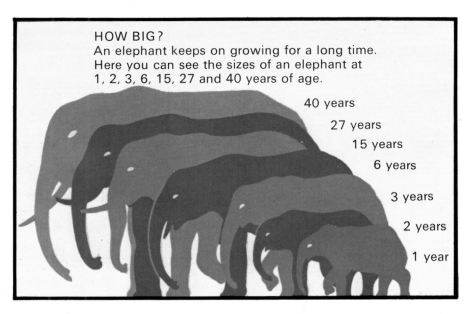

HOW BIG?
An elephant keeps on growing for a long time. Here you can see the sizes of an elephant at 1, 2, 3, 6, 15, 27 and 40 years of age.

40 years
27 years
15 years
6 years
3 years
2 years
1 year

Asian elephants are often used as work animals. They are good workers because they are both intelligent and strong. Elephants are experts at lifting and stacking heavy logs.

Indian elephant

hyrax

A TINY RELATIVE
Strange as it may seem, the elephant's closest relative is the hyrax, a little animal about the size of a rabbit. Hyraxes live in Africa, Arabia and Syria.

Life in the Cold

Many animals make their homes in the cold regions of the world. Most of these live in the Arctic. The mammals have thick, furry coats to keep them warm when the temperature is freezing. The Arctic summer is short, but the sun shines nearly all the time. Plants grow quickly. Animals such as the caribou move northwards to graze. When winter returns they move farther south to warmer places in search of food.

Some Arctic animals such as marmots and ground squirrels beat the cold by going to sleep for the winter months. This is no ordinary sleep, but a special kind known as hibernation.

When an animal hibernates its breathing and heartbeat become very slow. It needs very little food to keep it alive. Before winter starts the animal eats and eats until it is very fat. During the winter it lives on the fat stored in its body.

The musk ox (left) is nearly as big as a domestic cow, yet it manages to live off the thin grass and mosses of northern Arctic regions all year round. The caribou (below) and its European cousin the reindeer go farther south to find their food in winter.

musk ox

caribou

ermine

Many small animals, such as lemmings, voles and weasels, keep warm under the snow, feeding on the plants that grow there.

lemmings

voles

weasel

Adélie penguins

Very few animals live in Antarctica because it is much too cold. On land there are just a few spiders and insects. But the sea is a little warmer, and many seals and whales live in the Antarctic oceans. There are also many birds, including penguins like the Adélie penguins in the picture at the left.

Penguins cannot fly, but they are expert swimmers. They come ashore to lay their eggs and hatch out their young, crowded together in huge colonies. Penguins are playful creatures. They perform many funny antics on the ice.

fennec fox   red fox   Arctic fox   jack rabbit   hare   Arctic hare

Big ears help an animal to lose heat, and small ears to keep heat in. Animals that live in cold places have much smaller ears than those in warm climates. The fennec fox of the desert has huge ears, the red fox has smaller ones, while the Arctic fox has very tiny ones. The Arctic hare also has much smaller ears than its relatives of warmer lands.

The Arctic hare (below) and the ermine or stoat (left) have brown summer coats, but turn white to match winter snows.

Polar bears swim in the icy waters of the Arctic Ocean. They hunt for seals, walruses and fishes to eat.

A large bull walrus can weigh twice as much as a cow. It has a thick layer of fat to keep it warm.

polar bear

Arctic hare

walrus

The Bear Family

Bears are large, shaggy-furred animals. They eat lots of different kinds of food, including fish, roots, berries and small animals. Bears love sweet things. One kind in Malaya raids bees' nests for honey. Most bears are not dangerous to Man unless annoyed, but they can be very fierce when they are angry or protecting cubs.

The largest bear of all is the Kodiak bear of Alaska. It can weigh as much as ten men. The grizzly bear, which lives in the Rocky Mountains, is nearly as big.

Black bears are smaller than grizzlies. Most of them do not weigh much more than a man. They roam in many wild parts of North America. Another kind of black bear lives in the Himalaya Mountains of Asia.

The bears in the old fairy tales are European brown bears. There used to be many brown bears in the mountains and forests of Europe, but now only a few survive. Brown bears are related to the grizzlies and Kodiak bears of North America.

A polar bear smashes the ice around a seal's breathing hole. The bear waits at the hole for a seal to come along, and then pounces.

polar bear

seal

The polar bear is almost as much at home in the water as on land. It swims by paddling with its powerful front legs. It has hair on the soles of its feet, which help it to keep a grip when walking on slippery ice.

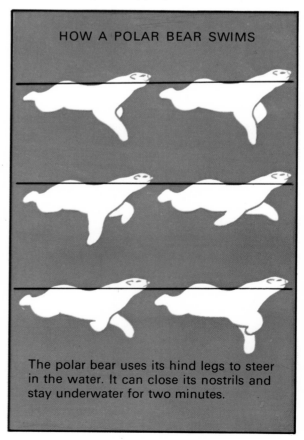

HOW A POLAR BEAR SWIMS

The polar bear uses its hind legs to steer in the water. It can close its nostrils and stay underwater for two minutes.

24

There is only one kind of bear in South America. It is called the spectacled bear because it has yellowish rings around its eyes. This bear climbs trees to pick and eat fruit.

If you explore the caves of Spain and France you may find the bones of the biggest bear that ever lived – the Great Cave Bear. The last one died about 20,000 years ago.

A black bear cub clings to the trunk of a pine tree. Black bears are good climbers. When danger is near, a mother bear will send her cubs up into a tree where they will be safe until the danger passes.

grizzly bear

spectacled bear

Bears come in different sizes. The biggest is the Kodiak bear of Alaska.

Kodiak

spectacled

black

grizzly   brown

A female brown bear has two or three cubs in winter, when she is sheltering in her lair. In spring she brings them out to learn how to forage for themselves. Often there is an older brother or sister with them, born one or two years before.

brown bear family

Giants of the Sea

Most of the world's fishes are small, but there are some real giants living in the sea. Some are fishes, such as sharks and rays. But the largest sea animals are mammals, which breathe air. The biggest of all are the whales, the real giants of the sea. These mammals never leave the water. Others, such as seals, spend part of their lives on land.

A fully-grown walrus can weigh 18 times as much as a man. The fur seal, unlike most other seals, has ear flaps on the outside of its head.

walrus

The common dolphin is a close relative of the huge whales.

bottlenose dolphin

The bottlenose dolphin has a long snout that is shaped like the neck of a wine bottle.

The swordfish's upper jaw ends in a long, sword-like weapon that can pierce the bottom of a small rowboat.

common dolphin

swordfish

Dugongs live in the Indian Ocean. They are often called sea cows because they "graze" on sea plants growing in shallow coastal waters.

sperm whale

Giant rays "fly" through the water by moving their wing-like fins up and down. Some rays are as big as 20 feet (6 meters) from wing to wing.

The sperm whale has teeth and hunts fishes. It can crush a small boat like matchwood.

dugong

giant ray

fur seal

sailfish

shark

remora's sucker

The remora is a fish that gets a free ride on large fish such as sharks. It uses a special sucker on its head to attach itself to the shark. The remora eats tiny parasites on the shark's body and leftovers from the shark's own food. remora

The sailfish has a huge sail-like fin on its back. Like its relative the swordfish, it lives in warm seas.

The great white shark can reach a length of 33 feet (10 meters) and is a ferocious killer.

blue whale

great white shark

The blue whale is the largest of all animals. Some blue whales weigh more than 20 elephants.

hammerhead shark

The hammerhead shark has an eye at each end of its blunt, wide head.

giant squid

leathery turtle

The leathery turtle is the largest marine turtle. Some grow to nearly six feet (two meters) long.

The two longest arms of the giant squid can reach over 40 feet (12 meters) in length.

Animal Oddities

Animals that live on islands are very often quite different from their relatives on the mainland. Slowly, over millions of years, they have changed to suit the places in which they live. Some of the most remarkable animals to have done this live in Australia, which is like a big island although it is really a continent. Australia is the home of most of the animals called marsupials, which rear their young in a pouch on the mother's belly. Their babies are very tiny when they are born and they need the protection of the pouch until they are bigger. The best-known marsupials are the bounding kangaroo and the little koala, which looks like a tree-climbing teddy bear. Both these animals look quite different from animals anywhere else in the world.

koala

giant tortoise

tuatara

Komodo dragon

The Komodo dragon of Indonesia may grow to 12 feet (3.6 meters) in length. It is the largest living lizard.

Some island reptiles: the giant tortoise lives in the Galapagos Islands; the tuatara is found only on some small islands off the coast of New Zealand.

A female red kangaroo with its young. A young kangaroo is called a joey.

red kangaroo

joey

Index

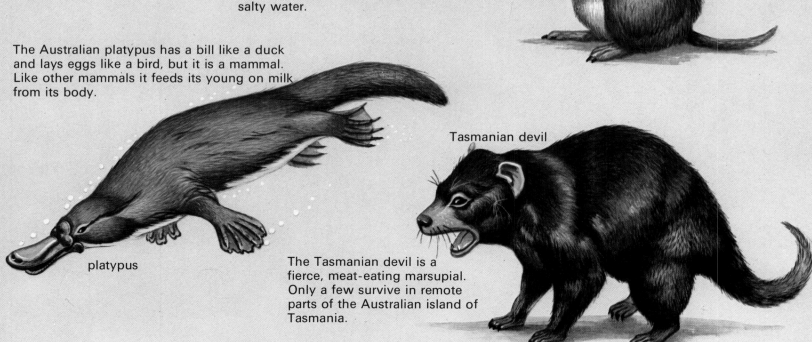

quokka

The quokka is a kind of kangaroo. It lives on Rottnest Island near Australia. There is no fresh water on the island, but the quokka, unlike most other land animals, can drink salty water.

The Australian platypus has a bill like a duck and lays eggs like a bird, but it is a mammal. Like other mammals it feeds its young on milk from its body.

platypus

Tasmanian devil

The Tasmanian devil is a fierce, meat-eating marsupial. Only a few survive in remote parts of the Australian island of Tasmania.